The
Courage
to
Be Free

ALSO BY GUY FINLEY

The Essential Laws of Fearless Living
Let Go and Live in the Now
The Secret of Letting Go
Apprentice of the Heart
365 Days to Let Go
Design Your Destiny
The Lost Secrets of Prayer
Letting Go a Little Bit at a Time
The Meditative Life
Secrets of Being Unstoppable
Being Fearless and Free
Liberate Your Self

For a complete list of the author's works,
visit *www.guyfinley.org,* where you can
also join the free Key Lesson Club to
receive weekly insights by email.

The
Courage
to
Be Free

Discover Your
Original Fearless Self

GUY FINLEY

WEISERBOOKS
San Francisco, CA / Newburyport, MA

First published in 2010 by
Red Wheel/Weiser, LLC
With offices at:
500 Third Street, Suite 230
San Francisco, CA 94107
www.redwheelweiser.com

ISBN: 978-1-57863-475-0
Library of Congress Cataloging-in-Publication Data available upon request.

Cover and text design by Maxine Ressler
Typeset in Mrs. Eaves
Cover photograph © Kenneth Munzlinger/iStockphoto.com

Printed in the United States of America
MV
10 9 8 7 6 5 4 3 2 1

The paper used in this publication meets the minimum requirements of the
American National Standard for Information Sciences—Permanence of Paper
for Printed Library Materials Z39.48-1992 (R1997).

Contents

What You Will Learn from This Book

Do you have the courage to be free? Not to just *wish* for freedom, but to meet every moment knowing that you have the right and the spiritual might to live without fear, worry, and doubt?

If you've ever really tried to shake off what's shaking you in some moment of unwanted change—then you know what you're up against. To cherish and long for the idea of freedom is one thing; but to find the courage it takes to let go of all that's keeping you from being free . . . seems that's another story altogether! Yet, freedom can be yours. Of this there's little doubt, provided you're willing to learn the truth about yourself—about who and what you are *not*.

For instance, you are *not* that sense of inadequacy that wants you to quit or give up on your life's dreams.

You are *not* that compulsive feeling that causes you to fawn before others in order to win their favor.

You are *not* any of those dark memories that swarm and sting you with sorrow and regret.

The truth is that you are not any of the defeated thoughts and feelings that try to drag you down and drive you to seek yet another new "power" by which to save yourself—again! And when you see the truth of these facts, your eyes are opened to a holy order of truth: You don't need new powers to find freedom. All such "paths to power" lead nowhere. Realizing the spiritual freedom you long for appears by itself once you *stop agreeing to see yourself as powerless in the face of punishing thoughts and feelings!*

In *The Courage to Be Free*, you will make the glad discovery that who you really are, your original fearless Self, can no more be made a captive of some unwanted situation—inward or outward—than sunlight can be made to stand in its own shadow.

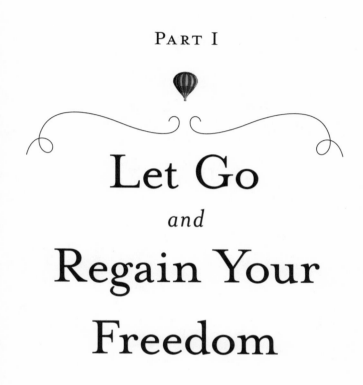

PART I

Let Go

and

Regain Your

Freedom

CHAPTER 1

Uncover the Treasure of Your True Self

EVERY SAINT, SAGE, and wise man or woman from every timeless tradition—East or West, past or present—has a special message for you:

You have been left a great inheritance.

A treasure chest of spiritual gifts awaits you; you need only claim it for your own. But this is no ordinary treasure; within this great chest lie others—chest within chest within chest—each one holding a prize that increases the value of the one before it! But let's not get too far ahead of ourselves. We'll talk about what's in the other chests once we've examined the contents of the main one.

Here's what awaits you in the first great chest:

Your birthright to be free.

Let's pause to consider the magnitude of this gift, keeping in mind how often we step, unaware, into the small prison cell of some self-compromising thought or feeling.

One thing we already know is that worry, doubt, resentment, and fear—whatever their shape or form—hold captive anyone unwary enough to fall into their web of woe. But your reclaimed birthright authorizes you to be as naturally free of these negative states as it is for you to be full of "grace under fire," regardless of how dire circumstances may seem. And there's more.

Yours is also the right to effortlessly recognize and release anger and frustration, to be able to see them for exactly what they are—false powers disguised as helpful guides in times of duress. And taking their place—as flowers replace weeds in a well-cared-for garden—are new powers of kindness, patience, and love. These characteristics are born of a living light that gently sweeps away whatever remains within you to oppose your liberation.

And what about the remainder of your yet-to-be-opened chests—the ones holding the rest of your inheritance?

Well . . . I don't want to spoil it for you. But in these unlocked treasure boxes, you'll find the rest of the new spiritual knowledge you'll need to reclaim the rights belonging to your original Self. Here's a partial list of these remaining gifts:

1. Unshakable faith in the goodness of life.

2. Perfect confidence that all things are fair and just, in spite of temporary appearances.

3. An effortless relationship with an order of reality whose timeless ground is the nature of success itself.

So now, let's actually open the first of your spiritual treasure chests. It's time to start gathering the facts we need to reclaim our lost legacy of freedom. We begin with a short story, a parable as full of surprises as it is with ways to prove this promise:

You have the right to walk through this life without any fear of what may await you ahead.

CHAPTER 2

Shatter These False Beliefs and Be Free

ONCE UPON A time, there was a wise old owl whose name was Solomon. As was true for the rest of his kind around the world, his duty was to take daily flights over the countryside where he lived in order to watch over the well-being of all the creatures residing there. Part of his responsibility, when needed, was to mediate the conflict that sometimes appeared between the various species and restore the balance of nature's harmony as soon as possible. Although the quarreling parties didn't always embrace Solomon's wisdom right away, they all knew that anyone who had the power to see into and through the darkness was someone worth listening to in times of confusion and conflict.

Now it happened that, early one fine September morning, Solomon was flying low over a particular valley that he hadn't visited for some time. From his elevated vantage point he could see that the colorful finger of autumn had already touched many of the treetops, and that the salmon were swimming upstream, returning home to spawn. Soon the riverbank feasting of the bears would begin, which also meant the gathering of eagles, crows, and the occasional ever-squawking gull. He took in a deep breath of the cool air, grateful to be alive and thankful for the deep silence of the open skies.

Solomon loved this part of the country. The dark green valley floor sat at the foot of a great mountain. Runoff from its snow-capped peak fed the river and streams that meandered through the forest and open fields beneath it. Flying high above the harmony of this world below, everything seemed in place and at peace. But just as he was about to bank his wings and fly a little farther south, something caught his eye that he couldn't quite make out and that made no sense at first glance. Making a slight adjustment to his course with a small turn of his head, he came back around for another look. He couldn't believe his eyes!

Walking along in a single file line, like soldiers on parade in a marching drill, were five great golden eagles.

Now this behavior was not all that unusual in itself, and might not even have caught Solomon's eye, were it not for one strange and otherwise inexplicable fact. All five of the eagles were wearing crash helmets, eye goggles, and raincoats!

"What on earth?" thought Solomon to himself, as he circled lower to confirm what his unblinking eyes couldn't believe. But sure enough, it was true; not only was each of them wearing what he thought he saw the first time, but slung over their wings were some kind of small flight bags! And so, in a nearly silent landing, Solomon set himself down directly in front of the parading eagles, greeting them with these few words: "Hello friends . . . how are all of you doing today?"

After a moment or two of awkward silence, the lead eagle spoke for the rest of them: "Thank you for asking, old owl; everything's fine as it can be." And, as the other eagles bobbed their heads in agreement, he continued. "To what do we owe this visit, if you don't mind me asking?"

"Not at all," said Solomon. "To tell you the truth, it's been a couple of months since I passed through this part of the country, so I was just doing a little flyby when I happened to look down and see the five of you walking along with all of this . . . gear."

He intended the pause at the end of his last comment to act as a question, hoping it would evoke an explanation for their strange behavior, but no such luck. All that followed was another short stretch of strained silence. Solomon decided on a more direct approach. . . .

"Look, friends, far be it from me to interfere in your lives, but I couldn't help noticing something strange going on here." Then, speaking in a deliberately softer voice—so that they understood he wasn't challenging them in any way—he finished his thought.

"Aside from the fact that you're all *walking* where you're going, which—you must admit—is unusual given how easily you could just fly there . . . don't you think it's a *little* odd that you're all wearing flight gear, not to mention carrying bags as well?" Solomon opened his already large eyes even wider in an attempt to show his genuine concern for their situation, but no one seemed to notice, so he just asked straight out:

"Anyone care to let me know what's going on here?"

Let Go and Regain Your Freedom

Making no attempt to disguise the irritation in his voice, the third eagle in line stepped forward to speak out. "What do you mean, 'what's going on here?' Isn't it obvious?"

But before Solomon had a chance to answer, the fourth eagle chimed in with an edge to her voice as pointed as her yellow beak. "We're on our way to our favorite riverbank to scavenge what's there, and to catch whatever else we need. *That's* where we're going, if you must know!"

"So let me see if I understand this," said Solomon, using one of his broad wings in a sweeping motion to gesture at their equipment. "Wearing and carrying all this gear, you intend to walk over a mile to your favorite fishing spot? Is that what you're telling me?"

"What . . . are you deaf *and* blind, old owl?" the lead eagle snapped back, making it clear the conversation was over. "*Leave us be!*"

Now, from his earlier encounters with them, Solomon knew that the true character of golden eagles was to hold equal amounts of patience and power—it came with their natural birthright to soar freely through open skies. So this intolerance of his friendly questions, coupled with their odd new possessions, told him two things for sure: Something had gone terribly wrong somewhere, and his task was clear. He must discover what had so compromised these magnificent creatures.

A moment later, Solomon spread his great wings and, lifting himself silently into the air, left only these last words behind him: "If you care to wait here for me, I'll be right back! Otherwise," he continued, " . . . don't worry; I'll find you, wherever you are." The five eagles looked briefly back and forth at one another, sharing an unspoken question: What on earth is this old owl up to? A heartbeat later, as if on cue, they took their respective places back in line and started walking again toward their favorite fishing spot.

As Solomon took off, his thoughts flew with him. Someone or something had successfully acted to take away the eagles' freedom *without them even knowing it!* So he knew that his first task would be to solve this mystery, and then to help them see the truth of their sad situation. But where to begin his search?

As he climbed higher into the bright afternoon skies, his thoughts became clearer. Instead of wondering who or what might be to blame, he began asking himself *why* anyone would want to deliberately steal an eagle's natural right to flight? And then it hit him.

He banked hard to the right, heading south to a small, secluded section of the forest glen where he knew the crows of that valley loved to gather and carry on. As he approached their meeting place, he slipped into stealth mode and landed, unnoticed, near the top of a distant tree. Even at this distance, he could hear everything the crows were caw-caw-cawing about, and by the arrogant tone of their voices his earlier intuition was confirmed.

It wasn't that Solomon didn't like crows, because long experience had taught him that every creature, regardless of character, serves a vital role in the beautiful unseen balancing act of life. It's just that crows were not his favorite creatures, given their penchant to profit from the work of others, and to otherwise steal whatever they couldn't win for themselves through their wily ways.

After listening to them for a few more moments, his initial suspicions were confirmed; he had the answers he sought. The crows were busy fighting among themselves for bragging rights over which of them was most responsible for having grounded the eagles! And then, the sound of a particular voice cut through the rest, catching Solomon's attention. He recognized it immediately. It belonged to Lucius, the self-proclaimed "King" of the crows and chief mischief-maker for more than 16 miles around.

"I have to say that, if I hadn't seen it with my own two eyes, I never would've believed it," said Lucius. "Whoever would've thought the great eagles could be tricked so easily?"

"What do you mean *who* could have imagined it?" cried one of the crows, hopping from branch to branch in an adjacent tree. "It was *my* idea, or don't you remember?" He paused just long enough to look from left to right, silently challenging anyone there to contradict his claim. "Yeah, that's right," he continued. "I told all of you that, once we convinced them that they really needed those special goggles to protect their sensitive eyes, getting them to believe they needed the rest of the gear would be a snap!"

"Blah, blah, blah," interrupted one of the larger crows perched about three branches below Lucius and his entourage. "Let's give credit where credit is due, or is this all about just *you*?" But he didn't wait for anyone else to chime in. He added, "Selling them the idea that they needed raincoats to keep their flight feathers dry—that was *my* idea. And throwing in the matching crash helmets," he continued to congratulate himself, "pure genius!"

But just then, yet another crow called out, eclipsing his moment in the sun. "Yeah, right. Sure they looked stupid enough in all that unnecessary gear, but aren't we forgetting the most important thing of all? *They were still in the air.* Day in and day out, they were still beating us to the best spots to scavenge for fish. So let's give credit where credit is due! They weren't *really* grounded until *I* convinced them they needed a shoulder bag to carry around their catch of the day."

He paused in his self-praise just long enough to look up and see that Lucius wasn't at all amused with his version of the story. And so, without missing a beat, the very next words out his mouth—as though they were what he had been leading up to all along—came as follows: "And of course, our victory over the eagles wouldn't have been complete without great King Lucius. It was *his* pivotal role that—*finally cooked their goose!*"

The crowd erupted in a spontaneous chorus of "caw-caws" at his play on words. While he waited for the laughter to die down, he was relieved to see the King was laughing too, so he kept going.

"Realizing that the eagles were no longer able to fly their usual overhead routes to our favored scavenging and fishing spots, our leader crafted an idea so clever that it will be spoken of for ages to come!"

Of course, everyone gathered there already knew exactly what had happened, but they cheered him on anyway. "Tell us, tell us!" chanted the crows in unison.

"Because of the extra weight they were now carrying, they were already walking instead of flying; but our great King knew exactly how to ground the eagles for good. So he had us convince them that, to find their way to the river and streams, they'd need to have with them, at all times, a special map. Then we told them that, out of his deep concern for their well-being, our wise King had just written the very book they required: *Eagles Walking Guide to the Best Fishing Grounds.*

With this, all the crows let loose, and the glen so echoed with the sound of cheers, clucks, and caws that the King had to demand their immediate silence.

"Quiet!" he said, sternly. "Keep your voices down! Right now, somewhere in this valley, the eagles are actually thanking us for what we've done to them. But if they ever catch on, if they ever discover our deception . . . it is we who are through!" He took a deep breath in order to enlarge his appearance, and then finished his thought:

"Yes, we've tricked them into surrendering their liberty, and that's good for us. But let's not fool ourselves. If we want to keep all that we've gained over these last few precious months, we must not let them learn the truth. Otherwise, we'll never be able to fool them again in the same way."

Solomon had heard enough! He understood why humans called such gatherings a "murder of crows." But now he had the facts he needed, and he felt certain that once the eagles learned the truth, their liberation was sure to follow. He deliberated for another moment, and then spoke out, revealing his presence to all of the crows.

"While it's clear to me why you have acted in this cruel and cunning manner, how can you believe that your plan will stand? This deception will be over soon, and with it will go your temporary rule over the eagles of this valley."

Solomon slowly turned his great feather-crowned head almost completely around, taking in all the faces of the dumbstruck crows. And no one knew, when he spoke, whether it was the sound of his voice or the dead silence into which he spoke that made his parting words carry for miles: "I leave you to yourselves, even as I fly to tell the eagles exactly what I have learned here this day. So, be warned. You have my promise. The truth I bring them *will* set them free!"

And the last thing Solomon heard as he flew out of sight was the sound of the thirty crows crying out in one collective, murderous tone: "They'll never believe you. They'll never believe you!"

CHAPTER 3

Recover Your Original Fearless Self

When Solomon had left the band of eagles, they were walking in the direction of a river all the creatures called "the Big Easy," but it took him nearly an hour of scouting the area before he found them again. As he dropped down to land on the sandy bank next to where he had spied them from high above, he could hardly believe his own eyes and ears!

All five eagles were engaged in a loud, talon-slashing squabble over the meager skeletal remains of a bear-shredded salmon. Solomon knew that, as a rule, eagles never fight with each other over what amounts to table scraps. Seeing them in this degraded condition nearly broke his heart—and may have clouded his judgment as well! Ignoring the injuries that could come from interfering with such infighting, he charged directly into their midst.

"Stop it! Just stop it!" he commanded them. And whether it was the authority in his voice, or the sheer audacity it took to step between them in the heat of their battle, they obeyed. But as shock gave way to angry disbelief that this old owl was meddling in their affairs again, they formed a circle around him and began closing ranks, hissing and lifting their wings in gestures of threat. But Solomon did not back down; in fact, he stepped forward. Taken by surprise, the eagles stopped in their tracks. For a moment, the advantage was his and he acted on it.

"Wake up!" he implored them, "For heaven's sake . . . Snap out of it!"

But, a scant moment later, as the eagles started moving in on him again, Solomon rebuked them even more forcefully. "*Look at yourselves.* Look at what you're doing here—to yourselves. *Can't you see what's become of you?*"

His words must have struck home, because, an instant later, the eagles seemed half their size, their aggressive spirit whisked away by a gust of wind that appeared out of nowhere. For many days now, all of them had been

Let Go and Regain Your Freedom

sensing that something was wrong, out of place. Un-explainable fatigue and frustration dogged them; they were at constant odds with each other, not to mention on the verge of starvation. Solomon seized the sudden quiet and began to speak.

"You already know there are creatures in our world whose interests are dead set against the best of your own." He paused to build on the point that would fol-low. "But what you don't know," he said, the urgency in his voice evident, "is that the crows living south of the Big Easy have conspired to deceive you . . . to defeat you. And to look at you now, it appears they've all but succeeded." He waited again to be sure his next words had the impact he intended.

"In fact, I've just come from one of their gatherings where they're all laughing at you. You should hear them bragging about how they managed to steal from you all that makes you unique, regal, and the masters of the sky. And, if you don't believe me . . ."

"Impossible!" the lead eagle cut him off. Then, seem-ing to catch himself, he backed off a bit as he continued his thought. "Yes, all right; it *is* true that the crows have been helping us of late, but don't you think we'd know it if they were deceiving us?" The other eagles bobbed their heads in agreement. "After all, we're nobody's fools!"

Solomon waited a moment, choosing his next words carefully. "No one would dare say otherwise. But just allow me a few simple questions and, if I'm wrong, no problem—I'm out of here. You won't see me again. But, if I'm right, then together we'll discover not only how you were tricked, but—by the light of our findings—the way to restore the freedom you've lost! Fair enough?"

The eagles' collective silence indicated consent, so Solomon began weaving his way through their ranks, inspecting them as would a general his troops. When he came to a stop, it was with his right wing extended and its leading feather pointing—like an accusing fin- ger—directly at the goggles atop the head of one of the eagles. But when he spoke, his question was directed to all.

"Were any of you born with these tinted goggles that now cover your eyes?"

Without waiting for an answer, he raised his other wingtip to point at the matching helmets covering their heads. "And how about these things? When you hatched from your egg, were any of you wearing protective helmets?" He thought this funny image might get a laugh from the eagles, but no luck. And so, with wings still outstretched, he continued walking among them, pointing as he went along.

"How about these rain suits, or your flight bags? And—oh yes," he said, reaching inside one of their flight bags, "Let's not forget this *fine* book of yours on how to find fish!"

At this point, one of the eagles stepped forward, making a halfhearted attempt to defend what was now starting to look a lot like an obvious mistake. "And your point is . . . ?"

Solomon didn't miss a beat. "You are created with eyes greater than those of any other creature. Neither they—nor your head—need protection in the open skies any more than a river needs to defend itself from raindrops. . . ." Shall I continue?" he asked, but he didn't wait for a reply.

"The natural sheen of your feathers can weather virtually any storm, which means covering them is not only unnecessary, but works to corrupt their waterproof nature. Your great talons, with their vicelike grip, are made to carry whatever you catch wherever it needs to go, without *ever* getting in your way. And within you already dwells a nearly perfect compass and knowledge of your domain. *No* map or book can ever better serve you as a natural guide than this innate wisdom with which you are born."

Then Solomon looked around at each of the eagles, making sure he had their full attention. He was ready to make his final point, and he knew everything depended on whether or not they heard the wisdom in his words.

"What I'm saying here is really *very* simple, provided you see the truth of it. None of this stuff you're hauling around with you is *original equipment*! The proof is right before us, right now—and you know it. What you thought would make your lives better *has only brought you down.* Yes or no?" A long collective silence signaled their reluctant agreement.

Solomon and the eagles spent the rest of that evening together, quietly talking into the wee hours about all that had been learned. The light and warmth of a small campfire comforted them in more ways than one, fueled as it was by all of the things the newly enlightened eagles knew they no longer needed.

Chapter 4

The Freedom to Change Your Experience of Life

To AWAKEN, RECLAIM, and possess the courage we need to be free, there are several important insights for us to take and study from this little story. First and foremost is this key lesson:

No negative state, no compromising or otherwise self-defeating thought or feeling, is your "original equipment."

In other words, who you really are, your original Self, doesn't come loaded with worry, regret, fear, resentment, or, for that matter, any other self-limiting states that can grow where darkness gathers. Let's make this perfectly clear:

No self-limiting thought or feeling—not one—is original equipment.

These feelings have power over us only when we are tricked into believing that we need something we don't—just as the eagles in our story were deceived into believing they needed all that "gear." When we let this happen, we begin to look at familiar negative thoughts and feelings as old friends; and though we want to be free of them, we still call on their powers to help us. We look to them to guide us, as when we walk and talk with worried thoughts, or when we embrace angry emotions for their short-term strength. But truth tells otherwise. In and of themselves, *negative states provide us with nothing of value.* Instead, they make victims of all those who seek their counsel. A short example will help prove this last important point and reveal how we are deceived into acting against our own best interests.

When life falls apart, or threatens to come unglued, it seems almost natural to carry around some desperate, stressed, or depressed emotional state. But why cling to something that makes us ache? The answer is surprising, but evident, once we're aware of what's actually taking place within us.

Negative states tell us that we must feel as we do.

In some strange and unseen way, the weight of a dark worry serves as proof that we have "no option" other than to buckle beneath it . . . to fall down, feel betrayed, or prepare for a fight. Which brings us to our next key lesson.

Real life can no more act to pull us down than the rising sun can burden the spring flowers that wait to bathe in its nourishing light.

Now we're going to prove this great and timeless truth. Each of the three special key lessons that follow are supported by four step-by-step insights designed to help you realize that your original Self is already free. The courage you need to prove this to yourself appears within you—by itself—with each glimpse of the new understanding that makes it possible.

Key Lesson 1:
No psychological fear is part of your original equipment.

Proof: You aren't born with a slide projector in your head—let alone one preloaded with unwanted negative images!

Insight: No psychological fear exists without negative imagination.

Explanation: No event, in itself, is the cause of the fear we feel in the moment of its appearance. William Shakespeare, whose insights into the workings of the human mind still remain treasures in spite of passing time, validates this important finding: "There is nothing either good or bad, but thinking makes it so." The same wisdom holds true when it comes to the moments that make up our lives: we meet in events nothing more or less than the wealth of possibilities they present before us.

It is the mind asleep to itself that makes monsters appear where there are none, just as a child's runaway imagination creates menacing shapes out of shadows on the wall. In this instance, we feel fear when our mind sees something that threatens us in some way. But what the mind that feels this *doesn't* recognize, but that we must see if we're to be free, is that it's looking at a negative image of its own making! This level of mind, divided

Let Go and Regain Your Freedom

and asleep to its *own creations*—then tells us what we must do to protect ourselves from its projection!

To give you a picture of how this plays out in a mind still asleep to itself, imagine a team of bogus bug exterminators, one of whom shoves termites under your back door, while the other knocks at the front door to sell you a service you suddenly need! Noted physicist and philosopher David Bohm sheds further light on this important insight into the nature of a divided mind:

> Whatever you think appears in consciousness as a show. That's the way thought works to display its content, as a show of imagination. Therefore if you think the observer is separate from the observed, it's going to appear in consciousness as two different entities.[1]

How does this new knowledge empower us to walk away from what's been hurting us? Imagine an artist who, as he sleepwalks at night, walks into his downstairs studio and paints a picture that, when he awakens the

---

1 *The Limits of Thought: Discussions Between J. Krishnamurti and David Bohm,* ed. Ray McCoy (New York: Routledge, 1999).

next morning, terrifies him. He's at a complete loss as to how this could have happened! So he buys an expensive security system, hires a patrol service, and takes a host of other steps to protect himself from an imagined intruder. None of these efforts work—and we know why! It isn't until he installs a motion-activated video camera that he catches the real culprit: *himself!* Shocking, for sure, but the outcome is wonderful. The artist's fear disappears in the very same moment he discovers its cause.

> **Your new action:** The next time some fear tries to drag you down into its world of worry— first showing you all that's dark and wrong, then telling you how to make things right and bright again—choose in favor of this action instead.

At the onset of any frightening situation—whether in the form of an actual event, or because of some worried thought that appears—remember that no such fear exists outside of the dream that makes it seem real. Then simply come as awake to yourself as you can, and *see what you're giving yourself to look at in that moment.* This new and higher self-awareness reveals the unthinkable:

Your own mind is scaring itself. As you see that the feel is real, but the "why" is a lie, you're done with both sides of the deception, and the dark state drops away by itself. This kind of clarity gives birth to a whole new kind of spiritual courage, for now you know that you don't have to free yourself from anything other than a misunderstanding about who you really are. And, by this same light, a promise dawns you couldn't have seen in any other way. You're already free; you simply have not yet seen the truth of it.

Key Lesson 2:
No painful resentment or regret is part of your original equipment.

Proof: You aren't born with a pre-filled photo album for a mind!

Insight: No resentment or regret exists without your being tricked into revisiting and reliving some painful mental picture from your past.

Explanation: The past is powerless over your original Self. Think about it. Does the echo of some spoken word have the power to change the voice that speaks it? Of course not. That which was "once upon a time"—regardless of its nature—has no authority over us in the present moment. The truth about the past is simply that *it has passed.* This means that our experience of each moment—for its pleasure or pain, peace or trouble—is a direct reflection of what we are in relationship with *in the present.* A brief example shows us the truth of this simple, but critical, idea.

Two friends go out to share a picnic basket on a warm, beautiful spring day. They spread their tablecloth over a soft rolling hill, taking their meal in the middle of an ocean of green whose waves are colorful flowers. As they dine, one of them looks out across the open meadow, drinking in the unspeakable delight of so much natural beauty. Giving her full attention to the rainbow of life revealing itself all around her, she thinks, "No one is more fortunate than I," and she wishes the whole world could know the peace and happiness flowering in her heart.

At the same moment, sitting less than three feet away from her—surrounded in equal measure by this living bouquet of spring flowers—her friend has a completely different experience! His attention is riveted on a horrible experience he had the day before. He can't seem to shake the image. In his mind's eye, he sees the face of his department superior, smirking with glee, telling him that he won't be getting the promotion he expected. And worse, it went instead to the new "hotshot" he can't stand, let alone that he'll now be working under this kid!

Here's the point. Although the man looks at the same open expanse of bright flowers as his friend, they see nothing in common. While she wishes everyone could know her joy, he wants only to escape his pain. But now *we* understand something that he has yet to learn about his own unwanted state. He is the unwitting captive of nothing but a self-induced dark dream. Improbable though it may seem, the bitterness he feels in reliving this moment is inseparable from his revisiting its emotion-packed memory. Life isn't punishing him; he is punishing himself by looking back at what he then wishes he didn't have to see!

Perhaps the day will come for this man when he grows weary enough of this kind of self-created conflict to realize the truth of his condition: the weeds of resentment and regret cannot grow in the light of any mind that knows what—and what not—to give its attention to.

Your new action: Our attention connects us to life; it establishes our relationships with all that unfolds around and within us. Our experience of life reflects these relationships just as a rainbow reveals the different colors of light. This means that, whenever resentment or regret darkens our day, there's only one reason for our sorrow: we've been tricked into revisiting and reforming an unconscious relationship with some misery-making moment from our past. We've simply made a bad connection within ourselves, due to a temporary lapse of attention.

If it helps, think of troubling times like these as your having been distracted while taking a long walk through the city. Maybe you were caught up with thinking about the "good old days!" Then you suddenly realize that, in your dream state, you've wandered by mistake into a dangerous neighborhood where you know that bad things happen all the time. What do you do? Do you stand there and hate yourself for having sleepwalked into a nightmare? Of course not! Awake now to the danger you've put yourself in—*and just get out of there!*

We can call on this same simple action whenever our attention wanders and takes us into the bad neighborhood of our painful past. In other words, if the resentful or regret-laden state we're feeling is due to a bad connection, we just deliberately disconnect ourselves from that dark thought by realizing where we are and how we got there. By reclaiming our attention—by bringing ourselves back into the present moment—we are released from our unconscious relationship with the past, putting its pain behind us, where it belongs. There's nothing more to it than that—other than to enjoy how good it feels to be free.

Key Lesson 3:
No anxiety—with its painful rushing around—
is part of your original equipment.

Proof: You aren't born with a merry-go-round in your mind, let alone with a lifelong ticket to ride!

Insight: No anxious state exists apart from the illusion that the security, happiness, and wholeness you long for exists somewhere outside of you—"in a time to come."

Explanation: Picture this. Someone you know and trust—a longtime friend—says to you, "Hurry up, come with me; I've just found what you're looking for! It's on the other side of town, but well worth the trip!" So you follow the friend, excited for his promise of what's to come. But, instead of taking you someplace new, he leads you into the park playground just across the street from where you live. A moment later he puts you on the merry-go-round and, as he walks away, leaving you to spin in circles, these are his parting words: "You're almost there . . . just keep going!"

How many times would you follow a "friend" like the one in our story? Someone who promises you the moon, but who leaves you holding old cheese? Suddenly, the wisdom of this old saying seems obvious: "Fool me once, shame on you; fool me twice, shame on me!" Once the truth of any situation is clear, so is our choice within it. No one consents to keep playing a part in a deception that, instead of delivering happiness, actually prohibits it. True enough, right? Then why do we go on embracing anxious thoughts and feelings that do nothing but steal from us our love of life? The surprising answer to this question is the same as opening the door to a life free of anxious thoughts and feelings.

Whenever our mind imagines a pleasure—going somewhere exciting, envisioning a new relationship, or picturing ourselves more successful than we've been—something else comes to life within us at the same time; right alongside our newly imagined desire is born a feeling of anxiety. We've all sensed the presence of this disquieting state, even though we're rarely conscious of it. At its outset, this fledgling anxiety remains largely unnoticed, and for good reason: Our mind's eye, our attention, is completely centered on the pleasure we imagine will soon be ours. But, in *real time*—in the reality of the moment—another story altogether is unfolding. Please follow the next few ideas closely to help you see the "big picture."

Regardless of whatever we imagine—be this some new happiness or sense of wholeness—*it isn't real.* If it were, we wouldn't have to try and dream it into existence! A closer examination of what happens to us when we place our hopes in "a time to come" reveals how we hurt ourselves without knowing it.

Can we see that there must exist a kind of psychological "distance" between any dream of a happiness to come and the part of us that dreams it up? It's true. There is an implicit, but *imagined* time and space between how we see ourselves in the present, and the happier person we will be "as soon as." And it's from out of this completely imagined distance that come all of our anxious feelings with their painful demands! After all, *before* we can know the wholeness we hope for, we must act to close this imagined gap—and the sooner, the better. After all, so much seems to be at stake! Here's the point:

It's impossible to imagine a future *wholeness without feeling, in the* present *moment, strangely* incomplete—*as though we're missing something essential!*

We've all sensed this disquiet each time we devise some new plan to feel "better" about ourselves. It's a little like how much hungrier we suddenly feel when we imagine a special meal for later that day. Anxiety shadows all such expectations, as small fears tend to appear with new challenges. And, as this anxious feeling of being incomplete rises into our awareness, there comes with it a kind of pressure to hurry. We feel compelled to either pursue (or protect) what's been imagined, or risk losing our hope for peace and happiness! The deception is complete and—*bang*—the trap springs shut!

In the ensuing struggle to escape our escalating concern, we leap onto the merry-go-round of whirling thoughts and feelings, *hoping that getting on will get us off!* What happens next is too familiar. Round and round we go, rushing through and running over anything in our way, trying in vain to reach the wholeness we've imagined awaits us in time.

Your new action: As long as we stay present to ourselves, anxiety is powerless to hold us captive. Now let's learn how to act on this new knowledge and stay out of the grip of anxious thoughts and feelings.

The natives in the rain forests of South America designed a cunning trap to catch the monkeys that live there. They build a wooden box in which will be hung a piece of fruit known to be favored by the monkeys in that area. A little hole is cut in the front of the box, just large enough for a monkey's hand, but too small for a hand holding a piece of fruit to pull back through! The hunters then strategically place their specialized trap along the known trails, sit back, and wait for the unwary. This trap works almost every time because, strangely enough, even as the hunters approach, the monkeys won't let go of the fruit in their hands; in effect, they trap themselves! The natives need only walk up and bag their prize.

The only reason we ever feel trapped by anxious thoughts and feelings is that we just won't let go of the false idea that it takes time to know the strength and happiness of our original wholeness. Our unseen belief in this illusion creates the uncertain future to which we feel we must rush. And this same illusion sits behind all of the fears that stalk us as we pursue whatever we hope will complete us. For implied in the idea of always having somewhere to "get to" is the danger that if we don't hurry up and "get there" we'll miss out on the fulfillment we've imagined awaits us. But here's the truth that sets us on the road to freedom:

Your original Self is already timeless and whole; any part of us that urges us to look for a bigger, better, or brighter sense of Self outside the present moment is both the seed of deception, as well as its bitter fruit, anxiety.

Anxious thoughts and feelings are not there to help us reach the promised land. Instead, they keep us a prisoner in the world of their empty promises. The courage to see the truth of this fact is the same as the courage we need to be free . . . to consciously walk away from these impostor powers, regardless of how convincing they are that we can't live without them. After all, *who clings to their captors?*

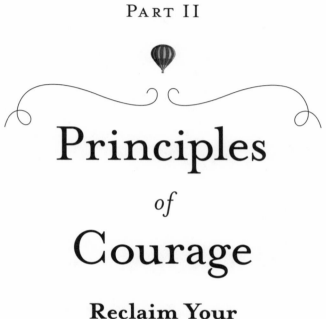

PART II

Principles

of

Courage

**Reclaim Your
Right to Be Free**

CHAPTER 5

Keys to Taking Command
of Your Life

WHAT IS THE value of being in command of our own
life? Is it that people applaud us for our strength of
character? Or that we've won the approval of our peers,
who think of us as being a "rock"?

When we are in command of our life, conflicts of one
nature or another may appear, but we can no longer
be tricked into compromising ourselves by mistaking,
for instance, resentment or anger for real strength, or
brash arrogance for quiet confidence.

When we're in command of ourselves, we don't say
cruel things to others. We won't rush. Fear can't make
a home in us. Painful regrets over days gone by become
a thing of the past; dark days lose their power to bring
us down because we now know the difference between

passing clouds and the skies through which they sail. *That* is true self-command.

Perhaps you're wondering if it's possible to know whether or not this effortless state of self-command actually exists. As you're about to see, the answer is yes. In fact, there's only one reason why we ever get dragged around by negative thoughts and feelings, and it *isn't* because they're too powerful to be put in their proper place!

The real reason we lose the command we long for may surprise you! It's due to a certain kind of spiritual "forgetfulness" that we'll define as follows:

In our moment of need, we can't remember the part of us that can't be made to serve anything not of its own choosing.

As simple as it sounds, we regain real command whenever we can remember this truth. Stirring ourselves out of the spiritual slumber into which we have fallen is the same as awakening from whatever dark dream may have been dominating our mind the moment before. Let's study this new and unusual idea, and find out why it works when all other approaches to self-command come up short.

Even though we all know the harm it does to lash out at others, to launch an angry attack or act with cruel intent, we still tend to do these things anyway. The following insights help make clear why this happens to us and how we are made, in effect, to act against ourselves and those we love without really knowing why.

Whenever we are threatened in some way, our tendency is to go into an "auto-respond" mode of behavior; certain habitual reactions rise up and effectively "take over" our thoughts and feelings. So, in a manner of speaking, it isn't really our true Self that meets these unwanted events. If we take a step back and quietly observe ourselves through impartial eyes, here's what we'll see is actually happening within us: We are being told how we feel, what to do, even who we should be *by what we're being given to remember in these moments.* Let's look at an example to help clarify this important discovery:

Whenever we act cruelly toward another, it's because something cruel "takes over and handles" the moment for us by doing what *it* remembers to do. In a manner of speaking, a state of cruelty imposes its rules on us, and makes of us what it will in the next moment. Much to our regret, we don't remember that any better solution exists until we have to deal with the grief that follows from having forfeited our freedom.

What's the solution to this kind of forgetfulness? First, without judging ourselves, we must acknowledge the truth of our present (psychological) situation; facts never lie. We are reacting to life's challenges from unconscious parts of ourselves that literally hand us a script and then direct us to play out a painful role. We are not meant to live like this—as real-time prisoners of our own pasts, captives of conditioning that serves nothing but its own continuity. Within us, awaiting our awakening to it, lives a level of Self that cannot forget what is right, bright, and true, any more than the sun can forget to shine each day. Let's prove the truth of this invaluable idea.

Who among us hasn't known times when we saw the truth of something and, in the light of that moment, thought, "Aha! I always knew that was the truth, but I forgot it." And it is right to say, "I forgot it," because we can see in those same moments that our "new" understanding isn't really new at all! We see that we *always* knew that truth, and that now—due to fortunate circumstances— we recognize it again! Let's summarize briefly:

Living within us dwells an order of being that knows, *without thinking about it*, what is authentically good for us and others. The problem isn't that this higher level of being—with its natural, calm command—is actually missing just when we need it most. The real problem is that we forget it! We forget that it's our right to remember what we want to remember, instead of what we are being given to remember!

Here are three spiritual principles designed to help you remember and restore your natural self-command. Allow them to remind you of what you already know is true and see how much easier it becomes to do what is true in the face of difficult moments. In no time at all, your anxious search for self-command will fade away as surely as shadows flee the midday sun.

**There is no intelligence in any fearful
or worried thought or feeling.**

What happens when we allow worried thoughts or feelings to tell us what to do about our problems? More worried thoughts and feelings follow! Why? Because we're listening to negative thoughts and feelings that tell us what to do about the darkness that's all around us. This is like trying to get out of a cave and back into the sunlight by following a bat! We must remember that there is no intelligence in any worry, anger, or fear, and then have the courage to act on our understanding. Let's take an example.

Perhaps you get some unwanted news at work, or your wife mentions some concern at home. All of a sudden, a flood of anxious thoughts washes through you. What if, in that moment, you could remember what you want to remember, what you know is true? What if you could remember that there is nothing good, no saving grace in the embrace of any worry or fear? Wouldn't your timely ability to remember this truth help you dismiss any of the fears that want to steal your self-command? Of course! By the grace of this same remembrance, the painful need to chase after a way to regain command of yourself disappears, because you didn't give it away in the first place!

No negative state has the right to rule over your life.

When things don't go the way we want them to, our tendency is to turn negative on the spot. It's as if something in us throws a switch and, the next moment—like being caught in the surge of a tidal wave—resistance carries us away. But this unconscious resistance to reality never shows itself for what it is; it can't, or the show would be over! After all, *who sides with something that is perpetually against life?*

Resistance is the unseen father of all lingering negative states. It derives its power to trick us into embracing its painful presence by a kind of misdirection. It hides behind a host of associated images that always appear with it—certain thoughts and feelings that promise either to protect us or to provide us with plans to escape our situation. But we must learn to see that the true nature of anything—whether a newly opened leaf or a fearful thought or feeling—is inseparable from what it serves. So, regardless of how it may appear, any disquieting state in us that "says" it wants to lead us away from a fear is leading us *toward* one instead.

Here's the main idea: *Resistance is negative attraction!* We bind ourselves to what we don't want! You can demonstrate this unwanted result for yourself by trying to push one hand away with the other. This action only forces them closer together, increasing the pressure between them. This means that the first step in releasing ourselves from the strain of this self-wrecking relationship is to see that we have unknowingly attached ourselves to it! The key is to have the courage not to resist, and to remember that what *you* want is release.

Pain is neither a natural nor necessary part of making a mistake.

There is a very surprising reason why we tend to suffer over our mistakes as we do. The real source of our pain in these moments—whether we're alone or with others —is the fear of being seen as less than we've imagined ourselves to be. We all know how it feels to try and save face, to scramble for scraps of lost dignity. But fearfully trying to cover up a misstep is not the same as knowing where we're going. In fact, whenever we feel compelled to cover our tracks, something is in command of us, isn't it? But here's the real question: What part of us wants us to believe that a good "cover-up" is the same as being right? The answer is surprising: It's our "un-original" self . . . a level of being that only knows itself through a slew of acquired social images, including the false belief that they must be protected at all costs.

Though we have yet to see it, beating ourselves up after making a blunder doesn't mean that we actually knew better than what we just did—nor does this kind of suffering lead to greater command or better decisions the next time around. Self-punishing acts prove only one thing: Something in us would rather suffer over what happened in the past than be present to those parts of us that erred in the first place. Real self-command dawns within us as we realize that *reliving the past is powerless to change a present misunderstanding;* it comes from the light of our new knowledge that having the courage to drop the level of Self that keeps wronging us and others is far more important than being seen as right. This same realization also grants us the courage to start life over—again and again.

CHAPTER 6

Act on What You Know Is True

TRUTHFUL PRINCIPLES CAN only act as agents of change for us when we choose to enact them. Their capacity to restore self-command, grant us a mind at peace, or deliver us from fearful dark states is only as great as our willingness to call upon their powers. That's why we must do the personal work it takes to put higher principles into practice. Napoleon Hill, one of the early great pioneers of personal development, asserts: "We can become complete masters of ourselves, if we so desire. The main thought to hold in mind is first to gain the knowledge, and secondly to act upon it."[2] And then act upon it! Wisdom is the seed of freedom, but only in action do we see it flower.

---

2   Napoleon Hill, quoted in Lillian Eichler Watson, *Light From Many Lamps*. New York: Simon & Schuster, 1951.

Study the special lessons that follow closely. Welcome their insight by allowing the wisdom they contain to remind you of their corresponding part in your own consciousness. Little by little, but surely as the acorn becomes the oak, you will know and grow into their power. New courage will flow into all of your actions, and the change will be unmistakable. Instead of reliving old reactions that take you nowhere, your path will become one of ceaseless transformation. And the fuel that drives this upward spiral of self-renewal is simple. You are learning to act on what you know is true about negative states, instead of allowing them to tell you what is true about *you.*

1. Understand that any lingering sense of discontent belongs to an inconsolable level of Self *that believes it can escape its pain by reliving it.* Giving yourself over to this kind of unconscious suffering is like falling off a boat at sea and hoping that a great white shark will save you if you promise to feed it a small sardine. You *know* what happens next! Now, have the courage to *act on this knowledge:*

Refuse to ever again hand yourself over to a nature that loves to complain about its circumstances, even as it does nothing to change them. Your reward: being released from the false belief that dark thoughts or feelings have any power to improve your life.

2. Understand that there are parts of you that always want to take the easy way—to do things halfway, to avoid unnecessary challenges, to coast whenever possible and pedal only as needed. Now have the courage to *act on this knowledge:* Deliberately choose to take the more difficult path and finish whatever you start. Walk into what you'd rather walk away from, and persist with what you know is true for you until all resistance to your new actions proves itself a lie. Your reward: discovering that on the other side of the resistance is the flow that always takes you, effortlessly, beyond yourself.

3. Understand that being anxious—rushing to or through things—does nothing but drive

you nowhere faster! When you find you're in a mad rush, remember that what you're really trying to get to is a quiet mind—that peaceable state of your original Self reached only through this realization: There's no place more empowering for you to be than in the present moment. Now have the courage to *act on this knowledge:* Deliberately slow down your life. Dare to stand directly in the stream of your own rushing thoughts and feelings—instead of allowing them to carry you away. Your reward: the deeply refreshing realization of what it means to be "washed clean" of anxious states.

4. Understand—in spite of the highly polished performances to make you believe otherwise—that everyone you meet suffers in much the same way as you do. No one wants others to know the weight of their unspoken pain. And yet, all are burdened with broken dreams, shattered hearts, and whatever other sorrow walks with them through their day.

Now have the courage to *act on this knowledge:*
Refuse to ever again add to the pain of
another, even a small measure of your own.
Whatever suffering you agree to shoulder in
this way not only helps to lighten the load
of those in need, but also serves to awaken
within you the strength you need to be a real
"friend in deed." Your reward: the birth of
a whole new kind of compassion that not
only flowers when faced with the weakness
of others, but whose fragrance helps heal
all those who are touched by it. Always
remember:

Your original Self cannot help but act from what is right,
bright, and true any more than the sun has to remember
to shine each day.

CHAPTER 7

Start Seeing the Good When Things Look Bad

MORE OFTEN THAN most of us care to tell, we run into unwanted moments that seem to challenge the very fabric of our being. Almost anything can be the proverbial straw that breaks us: a friend's betrayal, loss of health or a loved one, unexpected financial strain. Even a shattered dream can throw us into a dark nightmare. Certainly, no one gets out of his or her bed in the morning thinking, "Today I hope to encounter impossible circumstances!"

It's well known that storm-tossed waves often expose new treasures along the shoreline; there is unexpected wealth to be collected by those who know the secret value of rough seas. And yet, even though most of us have little tolerance for anything that "rocks our boat," the truth of the matter is self-evident:

Unwanted moments introduce us to parts of ourselves that would otherwise never get healed were it not for the difficulties that first reveal them and that lead us to release their pain.

The problem is that, when things go "badly," we tend to do battle! Hoping to put right what's perceived as having gone wrong, we work to rebuild our former sense of self by struggling to restore what life has washed away. But each time we resist life in this way, we miss uncovering a new and fearless understanding that is the greatest treasure of all:

The only reason life changes as it does is to reveal the secret goodness underlying those same changes.

When things go "badly" for us, we're not intended to "return" to who and what we have been. To see the good in this idea, we must be willing to see that the pain in unwanted moments can either be a rock into which we crash time and time again—a tempest without termination—or that same suffering *can be used as an inflection point,* a place of real change that exists only when all seems lost. Let's look at a simple illustration to illuminate this idea.

Whenever the right two stones are struck together, a spark will appear; there is a flash of light. This same principle holds true whenever we "collide" with life. In that instant parts of us that we've never seen before are illuminated. For instance, who hasn't crashed into that dreaded moment when we realize that someone we love has had a change of heart toward us? Suddenly we see, perhaps for the first time, how painfully dependent we'd become upon his or her company or approval and—connected to that same fearful neediness—our willingness to compromise ourselves, to do whatever it takes to keep that relationship in place.

It's this "spark"—the light of this new and higher self-awareness—that is our *real* friend in unwanted moments. It reveals what is concealed within us, releasing us from the psychic bondage of serving what had been secretly limiting our right to live without fear. If we will fan this spark of inner light, embrace instead of resist what it reveals about us, it becomes a kind of spiritual fire—a higher level of awareness that will always help us to see the secret goodness in seemingly "bad" moments. In this way we discover that behind every bitter disappointment lives the presence of a sweet light whose power can turn any unwanted event into a new kind of victory not yet imagined.

Let me share three ideas with you about this strange and wonderful kind of spiritual goodness that seems to arrive in a package marked: "Caution! Contents under pressure!" Welcome this light into your life and you will learn to exchange resistance to unwanted moments for being receptive to the lessons they bring with them. Soon you will know, without taking thought, the greatest secret in the universe:

All things good come to those for whom the Good is all things.

1. Even though we may feel badly when we lose whatever we hold near and dear to ourselves, it is good to see that nothing in this world—or that we can imagine—is permanent. Learning to welcome events that foster this understanding helps liberate us from painful attachments to relationships, possessions, and of course, our own bodies.

What follows is freedom from all forms of false dependency and their attending fears.

2. Even though we may feel badly when our sense of self-worth is shaken by events, it is good to see in these experiences that any sense of Self derived through images, social powers, acclaim, or peer approval is not who we really are. Learning to welcome events that reveal this truth helps free us from the impossible task of trying to be all things to all people and strengthens our intention to realize our unshakable original Self.

3. Even though we may feel badly when we run into a limitation of some kind, it is good to see that, apart from the certainty behind our own pressing demands on life, nothing else stands in our way. Learning to welcome events that illuminate this new understanding reveals two key lessons about limitless living: The more we resist seeing our own limitations, the greater they

become! And when we realize this truth, we see that limitations are illusions: They exist only for as long as we resist going through what we must to prove them false.

There is an old proverb that goes something like this: "God never takes anything from us without giving us something greater in return." The task for those of us who seek the life divine—those who seek to live from their original fearless Self—is to prove the trust of this timeless idea. Through it, we are set free.

CHAPTER 8

Finding Forgiveness for Those Who Hurt You

It seems almost inevitable: At some point, somewhere in our journey, we feel betrayed by someone or something. A friend lies, a loved one dies, our favorite pet prefers the company of someone else, you name it. And regardless of who delivers the blow, something else seems inevitable: the feeling of having been "burned" never seems to fade away; out of the blue old hurts are fanned back into life by freshly rekindled resentments. We may even want to forgive and forget, but there's precious little we can do to free ourselves from this searing in our soul.

The reason it's so hard to deal with these unwanted moments and their dark repercussions is that we don't really understand them at all. Looking at what we've lost—or at what a friendship has cost from the stand-point of the Self that feels betrayed—it almost seems natural to go on being negative.

Yet, isn't this kind of resentment just what small children feel when a caring parent says it's time to replace something they love with something new that they'll grow to love even more? Time to toss out that old stick-pony and let your father teach you how to ride a real horse! For a while, the child may feel like a victim, betrayed in some way. But the parent knows the child is being handed the keys to a whole new level of life that he or she can't imagine. This temporary disconnect between the child and parent exists as it does for good reason: The adult can see *both* worlds at the same time—the child's old one, and the new pos-sibilities just ahead—while children see only the one in which they feel happy and secure.

In scale, this same principle holds true for us when it comes to our moments of loss. We may not yet see it as being so, but whenever unwanted situations come along—stripping us of some beloved attachment—it is the operation of one world acting upon another. There is our familiar world, the one we've always known—who and what we've been, filled with our preferences and possessions—and acting upon it is a new order of reality whose meaning is unknown at first, but whose secret purpose is to help us awaken to our own higher possibilities. But when in such moments—moments only these colliding worlds can provide, all we see is our resentment or regret—we lose sight of this spiritual gift that can be offered to us in no other way.

Yes, someone has hurt us badly. Yes, we feel rage and regret, and all the stormy emotions that attend such losses. But, as we're starting to see, there is another story behind those bitter feelings of loss and anger. We live in a world where our earthly relationships are intended to teach us about higher, spiritual realms . . . where worldly affection is meant to be a stepping-stone to higher love.

In this instance, when we are hurt badly, the higher lesson hidden in this trial is to recognize the time has come to let go of who and what we have been up until the moment of loss. And "how" do we know this is true? How can we be sure there is something good in the "bad" others put us through? Because if we understand that events in themselves have no power to punish us, then who's to blame for our pain when life changes *as it must?* The real culprit here is our present level of Self—literally wrecking itself—as it clings to what can no longer remain in our life . . .

Yes! It does hurt to be left behind, or to be lied to. Yes, we feel lots of grief and anger—those knee-jerk reactions that rush in and rule a heart that feels so wrongly compromised. But as long as we cling to the false idea that who we really are is meant to be defined by any "other"—regardless how sublime—we have no choice but to feel that we're being pulled apart when our relationships change—*as they must.*

There's a silver lining to this kind of suffering once we learn to see it! Strange as it is, how else could any of our secret attachments ever be realized and released . . . if not for the unwanted events that come along to reveal them! Each "troubling" event, seen properly, is the herald of a freedom yet to be known. With this in mind, here's the higher lesson that awaits us on the other side of any loss, if only we'll open ourselves to its healing.

In the spiritual worlds above us, *we are the other.* The man who came to own a successful horse ranch is—

and will forever have within him—the small boy who couldn't imagine anything better than his little stick-pony. Nothing real can be lost. Just as the seed must give way so that the sapling it holds can spring from it, with all of its greater possibilities, we must learn to let go of what was, so that what may be can grow in its place. Love never dies, but only changes its form and expression that we may see its example and willingly follow suit.

One last thought. Our anger and resentment toward someone who has hurt us do not prove that we loved, and they didn't. What our enmity really indicates is that we don't yet understand the true nature of love, or we wouldn't be ripping ourselves apart because someone tore from us something to which we had become attached. The hole in our soul that is created by any such loss must be left empty. If we let it be filled with negative states, we will never know the birth of a whole new order of love because there is no room for it to grow.

Chapter 9

Never Feel Sorry
for Yourself

One thing that makes it so difficult to drop feeling sorry for ourselves is how *real* it feels when we are full of self-regret. But any perception of reality that requires us to submit to any such self-centered suffering is always a lie! Here's just one of several facts to be revealed that will give you the courage to walk away from ever feeling sorry for yourself again. Study it until you suddenly smile!

> *The secret attraction behind self-pity—why it's so hard to set down—is that the part of us that feels like nothing makes the part of us that points out this nothingness feel quite special!*

Negative states, in general, are part of an interior conspiracy to produce the illusion that no choice exists for us other than to cave in to their punishing presence. But, in truth, it is not we who are without choice in such moments. Rather it is the negative state that has no choice but to disappear as soon as we remember that no darkness is greater than the light that reveals it. In our heart of hearts, we know the truth of this liberating idea because we've all seen the great law that sits behind it.

We know that love is greater than hatred, courage slays fear, and that what is light, bright, and good only shines the more for anything that tries to darken its way.

The key to dismissing the parts of us that love to attend "pity parties" is to blow out the match that lights the candles of bitterness before they become inflamed.

Here is another lifesaving fact, so welcome the healing it brings by being willing to see the truth hidden within it.

There lives nothing real in our past—regardless of how disappointing or painful it may have been—that can grab us and make us its captive, any more than dark shadows have the power to keep us from walking into the sunlight.

Now, add to this fact the realization that there is never a good reason to go along with feeling bad about yourself, and you're on your way to living in a world without self-pity. Call upon the following special key lessons to guide you as needed. Use them to help strengthen your wish to be free of all dark self-compromising states.

1. The only thing feeling sorry for yourself changes about your life is that it makes it worse.

2. No matter how you look at it, you involve yourself with whatever you resist!

3. Being wrapped up in self-pity completely spoils any chance of being able to see new possibilities as they appear. Besides, no one likes sour milk!

4. The only thing that grows from cultivating any dark seed of sorrow is more bitter fruit.

5. Feeling sorry for those who want you to feel sorry for them is like giving an alcoholic a gift certificate to a liquor store.

6. Your thoughts can no more tell you what is true about your possibilities than a set of streamside boulders can know the nature of the waters that rush by them.

7. Feeling sorry for yourself is a slow-acting poison. First it corrupts, then it consumes your heart, choking it with dark and useless emotions.

8. You cannot separate the reasons you have for feeling sorry for yourself from the sorry way you feel.

9. The heart watered by tears of self-pity soon turns to stone; it is incapable of compassion.

10. When you agree to live with sad regrets, you ensure they'll still be with you tomorrow.

One last thought. Before we can know a happiness beyond the reach of any sorrow, we must ourselves be whole, for any happiness apart from self-wholeness is only half a happiness and must, in time, prove itself so.

CHAPTER 10

Let Go and Flow with Real Life

REAL LIFE IS not static. Its only rule is change; so, it should be clear: either we agree to participate in the process of this eternal renewal, or we will feel punished by it. This means it's impossible to be someone who knows how things "should be"—and share in life's ceaseless newness at the same time. Yes, we may be able to devise a formula for a prescription drug, or create a delicious recipe for vegetable soup—but no system of thought that can stand up to the ever-shifting changes of real life, let alone meet those same changes fearlessly. Regardless how sophisticated its knowledge, the Self that knows itself only through its own conditioned thinking can never develop beyond the content of itself, any more than a math equation can suddenly outgrow the line of symbols responsible for its form.

The truth is we *can't* know what to do in advance of any given moment. When we meet life with preconceived ideas about how to respond to what unfolds before us—we are like downhill skiers trying to know when and where to make turns *before* it snows. Add to this idea the fact that whenever socially contrived ideals go before us as measuring sticks, they are too soon turned into some form of self-righteous judgment—making us quick to punish anyone found guilty of not doing what we think ought to have been done.

Knowledge, regardless of its sophisticated nature, is a tool. It arises from and belongs to what has passed. As such it embodies, defines, and relates us to life through what we already know is true about the world around us. By definition, this kind of understanding is limited. But *real life is not limited* to what was; it is always new because it's the expression of a compassionate and living intelligence that actively shapes whatever it touches, as well as whatever reaches out to touch it. You could say that each moment appears, as it does—in whatever its form or color—hard or soft, dark or light—*to reveal us to ourselves.* How can we hope to learn from such moments, to be transformed and perfected by them, if we meet them with hardened biased views about how they should unfold? No form is free.

And just as one wouldn't mistake the ladder he must climb for the rooftop from which he hopes to view the stars, neither should we confuse even the most sophisticated spiritual knowledge for those innermost revelations that can come to us only through living in the now. *Genuine self-knowledge is one and the same as being fully self-aware in the present moment.* As such, it is never static. This fluid level of Self places no demands on life, therefore it fears nothing that life may reveal. Being fearless, it never has to imagine a freedom "to come," any more than a river needs to imagine how to flow.

When you are present to yourself, quietly watchful of the relationship that is always unfolding in the present moment, then you have no more need to prepare for what life will bring than a newly opened rose needs to ready itself for the warmth of the sun that comes to release its fragrance.

CHAPTER 11

Being Friends with Truth

CAN YOU RECALL how, in younger days, your parents told you that they did not want you spending time with a certain person or group of people? The idea behind their concern was simple, even though perhaps you couldn't see it at the time: If you continued with that relationship—which they saw as being "bad" for you, nothing good would come of it!

Most of our parents either did not, or could not, explain to us why they wanted to restrict some of our relationships. The truth is, apart from their general understanding that "a bad apple ruins the whole barrel," our folks didn't have much insight into the timeless truths by which they tried to live. They just "knew" that trouble follows those who keep bad company. And Mom and Dad were usually right!

In fact, many years later, their wisdom then seems painfully obvious. If only we had listened! Dolphins do not swim with sharks; coyotes don't keep rabbits as pets. Life instructs us: lambs lay down with lambs. It's clear that all creatures have their circle of "friends," and that outside of the wise tolerances these relationships will bear, we all tend to keep company with those we are most naturally comfortable with. But there's more to this fact than our first glimpse reveals: just as we need to keep an eye on the kinds of friends we keep *around* us, so must we also remain aware of the circle of "friends" we keep *within* us—our own thoughts and feelings.

Not only does the largely unseen content of our mind and heart cause us to feel attracted to certain kinds of people and events, it also serves as an attracting agent for those who want to be around us. Personal experience proves the truth behind one of our most ancient axioms:

The inner determines the outer.

It's likely that most of us haven't taken enough time to think through how the nature of our thoughts and feelings determines the kind of company we keep. But

I assure you the truth behind this idea touches our lives in ways yet unimagined. Speaking of which, here's another timeless truth that underscores the importance of keeping good inner company:

We resemble those with whom we assemble.

Simply put, this means that both our appearance and character change according to the kind of company we keep. In other words, never a moment passes in which we are not being acted upon by those relationships that we share with people and things in that same moment. It's no accident of fate that people often look something like the dogs they love!

In much the same way, only with far greater implications, a mind full of worry and doubt can act to transform the human face into a fearful one—we see eyes full of apprehension, lips pulled back tight, the mouth turned downward. As we're about to discover, the implications of this finding are vast; seeing the truth of them will awaken the need in us for a continuing vigilance, both outwardly and within the world of our own thoughts and feelings.

Our experience of life is a creation of the ceaseless interaction of invisible forces that are always active around and within us. This means that continual transformation of Self is much more than just an idea. It is an eternal axis around which our life revolves, and through which our present level of Self is ever becoming—for better or for worse—more limited or increasingly limitless. The point should be clear:

What we are now, and the kind of life we will come to know, is very much determined by the "interior" company we keep.

Although this idea of "inner" company may be new to you, its reality becomes common sense once we see the truth of it. In this instance, we live in a perpetual relationship with our own thoughts and feelings. If it helps you to visualize this last idea, think of these thought forms and emotional forces as your invisible "circle of friends," for that is exactly what they are. Yet, they are more.

We know that every creation under the sun belongs to a certain order of being, and that these orders themselves are further classified according to the many levels of creatures existing within them. We also know that these various levels interact with one another according to their nature. This same principle of hierarchy pertains to our own thoughts and feelings. Most of us already know, intuitively, that love, patience, kindness, and compassion arise from a higher order of being than do negative states like hatred, frustration, resentment, and fear.

The wise ones of all ages—long called the "Friends of Truth"—understand, as we are now invited to, that the more time we spend in the company of these truly higher ideas, the more the life of these timeless truths becomes our own. Welcoming "friends" such as these into our lives grants us the power to "move mountains" because, with their guidance, we no longer make the mistake of building some "molehill" into an impassible barrier. These friends go before us to make the "crooked places straight"—by lifting us above the level of mind that creates one dark corner after another with its unconscious demands.

How does one become a friend of truth? As we're about to see, the answer is surprisingly simple. We must be willing to see the truth of ourselves, starting with this somewhat shocking revelation:

The things we put first in our life, our moment-to-moment choices in life, are a direct reflection of what we value most in that moment.

What this means is that our experience of life—for its pain or pleasure, darkness or brightness—is a perfect reflection of what we want most from life. People who want to go on feeling like victims despise truths like these; after all, it's so much easier to resist and resent our circumstances than it is to change the consciousness responsible for the way we perceive them. Prove this truth to yourself, and you will put out of your life all that presently limits it.

Let's take an example. We all have to drive places— work, market, school, whatever. We can just drive "there"—meaning get through the task—so that we can get on to the next thing we must do. Or, as we drive where we're going, we can be aware of the "rushing" thoughts and feelings that are driving us on. In other words, regardless of what we must attend to physically, a higher spiritual choice exists right there and then—*if* we choose to be present to it.

In this instance, even as we're busy going somewhere, we can work each moment to be mindful of the company we're keeping in ourselves, and whether or not we want to be friends with those pressurized thoughts and feelings that are telling us to hurry up and get there! By consciously choosing higher awareness as our friend, we can't be compromised into giving up our right to move at a speed of our choosing. No haste, no waste! Our new level of self-command is a direct reflection of the company we have chosen to keep in that same moment, and it's quite clear that it makes no sense to be friends with anxious thoughts and feelings. After all, who rushes around in order to get somewhere to rest?

This special kind of mindfulness—a willingness to observe your "Self" and to be honest about the circle of "friends" within which it runs—does two things for you at once. First, by putting the wish to see the truth of yourself before the act of trying to win what you want, you soon see that most of your desires and their demands are not the friends they pretend to be.

Rather, they are a host of small powers into whose hands you've mistakenly entrusted the keys to your consciousness. And further, that in exchange for this friendship you've given them, they have become—for all intents and purposes—tyrants dedicated to taking away your right to be self-ruling.

Continuing with this last idea, and perhaps most liberating of all is this second realization: Choosing to keep the company of truth is the same as choosing to lose all the false "friends" that presently limit you. Just as you can't cage a lion in a child's crib, no negative state can keep you its captive once you've seen it for what it really is—*nothing* without your consent.

Chapter 12

Step Out of the Rush and Into Relaxed Living

A FAMILY WENT to its favorite park for a Saturday picnic lunch. While the three boys, William, Paul, and Michael, played together, running up and down the green rolling hills as fast as they could, Dad put the finishing touches on the meal while Mom put out the paper plates on a checkered picnic tablecloth.

Suddenly, they heard the youngest child, William, cry out, as if in pain. A second later, they were dashing in the direction of the distant sound, unable to see any of the boys because the hills obscured any direct line of sight. When they arrived, they found Michael, the eldest, standing over William, who was lying on the ground whimpering.

"What on earth have you done to your brother?" the mother demanded of Michael. "I've told you time and time again not to pick on him!"

"But, I didn't," Michael protested. "That's not what happened!"

"Well, then," asked the father, "Why is he lying here crying like this if you didn't hurt him?"

Michael paused and looked over at his middle brother, Paul, hoping to find some kind of support. Finding none, he gathered himself and answered:

"We were all running up and down the hill, and while William was walking up, I was running down." Michael looked over once more to Paul, but he could see Paul was actually enjoying the moment.

"And . . . ?" Mom and Dad asked at almost the same time, seeing that Michael was stalling for time.

"Well, I guess on the way down I ran over William . . . and that's why he's crying . . . *but I didn't mean to . . .* honest!" said Michael.

"Then why did you trample over him?" asked the father in a tone that told Michael he wanted to hear the truth and nothing but the truth.

Principles of Courage

Michael paused to think over how to explain the incident and then, suddenly realizing exactly what had happened, spoke these words:

"I was just going too fast to stop," he said, "and . . . well, William just got in the way. I'm sorry, Dad, . . . Mom, . . . really, I am!"

We've all probably "run over" someone emotionally or hurt a friend, a loved one, or even a complete stranger while racing to get somewhere or do something "important." And, like Michael, we regret it—most likely too late to do any good.

There may be no greater self-deception than the false notion that rushing through anything actually helps us in any way whatsoever. After all, if anxious thoughts and feelings had any power to deliver us to a place or time where peace awaits, don't you think we'd have gotten there by now? Let there be no mistake here:

When it comes to being in a hurry, what difference does it make how fast you can get somewhere when all you find there is the next thing for you to rush through?

The following nine lessons contain special insights into the invisible pressure-filled states that cause human beings to run themselves ragged. The more clearly we can see that it's impossible to reach a place of rest by rushing to get there, the sooner we'll arrive at the true solutions that allow us to relax, slow down, and realize the relaxed pace of an inwardly liberated life. Study each of these lessons separately, but see them as telling one story whose happy ending goes something like this: You not only find the courage you need to step out of the rush, but you also awaken to a whole new order of yourself that gets everything done without you doing yourself in!

1. Anyone who rushes through life always finishes last! This is a truth unseen by the masses, but evident to those weary of going nowhere fast. You race as you do to escape the unhappiness you feel being where you are, running toward what you imagine will free you from that dissatisfaction. But such races are always lost before they begin because you can't outrun yourself!

2. All forms of momentum are mindless, but never more so than when a mind—blinded by desire—runs after what it wants without any awareness of its action.

3. Patience is a great virtue whose cost is paid by becoming painfully conscious of what our impatience does to others.

4. The rush to judgment is a race that nobody wins!

5. Allowing the rushed state of another person to push you into an anxious state of mind is like letting the horse you're about to ride convince you to wear the saddle!

6. You are well on your way to reclaiming your original fearless Self when you find your source of peace and contentment in just being alive.

7. Rushing through life lends the one who habitually hurries the feeling of being "important," but loans such as these come at the high cost of always having to justify one's

unkindness—like when we have to convince ourselves that our impatience with others is a necessary evil along the way to that "greater good" toward which we think we run.

8. The main reason it's wise to listen to one's own heart—whenever we can step out of the rush and remember to do so—is because there's much more to be learned from the parts of us that don't "speak" in words . . . than those that do.

9. The most important thing to remember whenever you find yourself in a mad rush is that what you are really trying to get to is a quiet mind . . . a peaceable state of Self reached only by realizing there is no place more empowering for you to be than in the present moment.

CHAPTER 13

Break Out of Any Rut

IT WOULD SEEM that the task of providing for ourselves and for those we love brings with it a certain kind of dissatisfaction. Most of us must go to work every day and perform repetitive tasks that are rarely of our choosing. And when these unwanted routines run—as they do—through our reality, it isn't long before our growing resistance to them leaves us feeling weary, if not burned out!

Even if we're lucky enough to make a living doing what we wish, what feels good one moment can become a grind the next; we all know the drill whenever we start feeling stuck. Resistance to our situation swells in us like a cresting wave, and moments later we're carried into a world without gratitude, enthusiasm, or hope. Now add to this sad scenario the fact that this resistance itself becomes a part of our routine, and it's easy to see why we often feel as if we're stuck in a rut!

Yet, not everything is as it seems. Looking at life through the eyes of resistance is not unlike looking at our own reflection in a pool of troubled waters; everything gets distorted. In fact, when seeing our lives through the narrow bars of some unwanted state, *nothing is the way we see it.*

Yes, it may feel as though we're stuck in some rut, but our original Self can no more get stuck in a rut than sunshine can be glued to the floor. So, the first step to releasing ourselves from any sense of being in a rut begins with seeing this truth:

The real nature of what we call our "daily grind" is really just our own mind telling itself, over and over again, how much it wishes things would change.

This brings us to this next important lesson. It comes to us in two parts, but tells one story much as an oak tree grows out of an acorn. First, our present level of mind can only place and hold its attention on one thought or feeling at a time. Secondly, as goes our attention, so comes our experience.

For example, we can see that whenever we give our attention to something beautiful—a field of spring flowers or robins romping in a birdbath—we experience within us the delight of what we've given ourselves to see. But as we're about to learn, this same principle holds true when it comes to how we make ourselves feel when looking at "scenes" in our lives that we don't want to see. Let's gather the details behind this important discovery.

When we feel stuck somewhere, in a rut of some kind, to what do we give our attention? As a rule, what we see in our mind's eye is the circumstance we think responsible for how we feel in that same moment. Although this pattern of placing blame on conditions outside of us seems wise, a closer look tells a completely different story. In fact, this way of looking at our situation is a part of the very rut we wish to escape! Remember:

No condition outside ourselves can create a rut or trap us in it.
It's impossible.

Use the next friendly fact to prove this important idea: Ruts don't create the cattle that follow them; cattle create ruts by blindly following one another, slowly grinding down the ground upon which they walk. If life seems like a grind, it's only because we're following around the same level of thinking that makes it so. Blaming outside circumstances for trapping us in a rut is like blaming the television for the boredom we feel while sitting watching nothing but reruns.

It's time to break our ties with anything in us that would rather complain about its situation than go to work to change it. And it doesn't matter where or how we feel stuck—whether we're living under what seems an impossible situation, making too many self-compromising choices, or feeling like a prisoner of what seems an inescapable past. Yes, our condition may feel real, but any reason our mind gives us about "why" we're stuck there is a lie! Great nature herself proves the truth of this when we know where to look!

Nothing in life repeats itself in exactly the same way: not the seasons and not the path of the stars that drive those seasons, let alone the eternal genesis that sits behind all of creation. More simply stated, *life never travels the same road twice.* Like a bed of roses bathing in streams of sunlight, not a moment unfolds when some new impression isn't raining down upon us, even as it wells up from within. So anytime it feels as if we're a captive of some condition outside us, this sense of ourself has to be a lie, because nothing in real life remains the same! Living in the grip of this illusion is like sticking our finger into a bucket of ice water on a beautiful summer day, then not wanting to go outside because we're sure it will be too cold to play!

So, the first step to breaking out of any rut in life is to no longer enable the parts of us that keep walking in them while wishing they weren't so deep! Learning to watch our own thoughts and feelings—to be quietly attentive to what the mind is attending to in each moment—ensures that we won't fall into these ditches, because our heightened level of attention keeps them from being dug!

We wouldn't allow a small child to wander around, unattended, in a working construction zone; in such a place, danger is everywhere for the mind that can't see it. Nor, for the same reason, should we allow our own mind to just go and do whatever it wants. Even though it remains largely unseen, life on earth is a kind of invisible construction zone, a ceaselessly active "creative zone," in which dwell a host of psychic forces, light and dark alike. The extent of their power to influence how we experience our life depends upon our awareness of them. Again, as goes our attention, so goes our experience.

Trying to reclaim our attention can feel, at times, like trying to pull a willful child out of line just as it is about to get on its favorite amusement-park ride. This interior struggle can be very difficult sometimes, because, as hard as it is to believe, there is a momentum to all things—including our misery over feeling stuck. Such misery doesn't just love company; it wants to continue with its life. Nevertheless, persist!

Remember. Each moment of reclaimed attention gives us a stake in the freedom it grants.

For encouragement along the way, just notice how, each time you bring your attention into the present moment, it's *you* who gets the gift of being made new. That's the way it works.

See how many times you can catch yourself just as you're about to go on the "ride" of not wanting to be where you are—of not wanting to do what you must. Then deliberately step out of that long line of repetitive thoughts and feelings. Take your attention off what you *don't* want, and bring it into the new moment—as it is.

This new and higher level of attention connects you to the present moment, the living *now* that is one and the same as your original Self. The interior task of working to remain attentive in this way grants you entrance into a world free of routine, without ruts of any kind—*because no one has ever been there before you.*

CHAPTER 14

Practice Living in the Presence Moment

DOING WHAT IS right for you, and for everyone else, begins with *remembering* that nothing good ever comes out of compromising yourself. So slow down and see that anything that wants you to act in haste—to lash out at another, or even at yourself—is to make two mistakes at once. First, you cannot act compulsively and be in command of yourself at the same time. Second, any part of you that pushes you to act against yourself in this way also wants you to waste the possibility of knowing your original fearless Self—the eternal part of your being that can no more act against itself than can a wave disturb the ocean deep. The following insights will help you to broaden and brighten the special self-understanding you'll need to gain entrance into this peaceable kingdom within you.

All of life's innumerable "shake-ups, breakups, and wake-ups" take place within what we call the "present moment." This ever-open window into life—through which we see the newness of life unfolding before us—is something much, much greater than all of the individual events that pass through it to reveal it. To help you visualize this important new idea, it may help to think of the present moment—and all that goes on within it—by considering the invisible relationship that exists between our great oceans and the rest of the waters found throughout the world.

In one way or another—over periods of time that may be unimaginable—the waters found in every lake, river, stream, pond, and raindrop come out of our ocean's body in one form, only to return to it again in yet a different form—and all in a cycle that's virtually eternal. From evaporation to precipitation—as fog that forms tiny dewdrops that become torrential waterfalls—all of these waters keep falling until they find their way back "home." So, compared to the ocean itself, whose body can be thought of as being relatively timeless, its individual waters are "in time"—meaning they come and go, appearing first in this form, and then in another.

Now let's use this new understanding of the secret relationship between the ocean and its waters to help us understand the deeper, hidden meaning of the present moment, and our real place within its endlessness. If you will quietly ponder these next new ideas, they will help you to see—and to start *being*—one with the timeless world within you.

The events in our lives constantly flow down to us from someplace "upriver" that seems guarded by a bend beyond which we can't see—a time we think of as the "future." And what we call the "present" is that all too brief moment of playing in these gleaming waters just before they disappear downriver—beyond yet another bend we call the "past." But if we could climb the mountain around which this river flows—rise high enough to see beyond its twin bends—everything about our relationship with life would be changed in the twinkling of an eye.

We would see from where these waters come, and to where they flow; and we would *know,* accordingly, that they have neither beginning nor end because they belong to a boundless ocean of timeless energy from which they came and will return—a single and celestial Life whose living waters are infinitely aware of themselves . . . forever. What we call the present moment is really our momentary awareness of this ocean of consciousness, a self-aware *Presence* of immeasurable power, and more.

The Presence moment can be thought of as a kind of "meeting" place of myriad invisible worlds. It is a timeless space of open-ended possibilities in which your created nature converges and interacts with all that constitutes your original Self. Call this all-encompassing Spirit what you will, but it is . . . and forever will be a compassionate intelligence whose living light creates, animates, and sustains all natures, including our own.

Our created nature can be thought of as a collection of interactive forces that have not only helped to shape our existing persona, but continue to mold it according to a host of acquired preferences. To carry this idea one step further, where our created nature meets and interacts with this Presence can be called the "moment" of our destiny. From this ceaseless marriage springs the seed of that union, with all its new promise and rich possibilities.

Until now, we've had little choice in how these "seed moments" unfold, because our present level of Self—with its accumulated fears, compulsions, and doubts—knows only one way to deal with the disturbances that upset its precarious balance. It thinks about them. It calls on the body of its collected past experiences, compares them to its current situation, and then concludes both the nature of the problem and what must be done to "deal" with it.

But this much should be clear to us by now: Looking to the past for guidance on how to make a new beginning is like asking an echo to show you where it got started. Which brings us to an important point: We do not need to think in order to know the right thing to do in the moment for ourselves, or for others! In fact, quite the opposite is true.

The amazing possibilities that appear with each present moment are literally *beyond thought.* After all, as the following examples reveal, the best moments in our lives—those priceless times when we feel most alive—unfold without our taking a single thought about them. Of course!

That unforgettable sunrise we shared with someone we love; some deep heartache released and our soul refreshed on the heels of some unexpected insight; better still, a beauty beyond words when we turned a corner to find a field of yellow flowers flowing alongside a stream. In moments like these, our sense-dominated mind comes to a full stop, because it stands in the presence of a delight beyond its capacity to contain or otherwise restrain by thought, At times like these, we are left, gratefully, in the living presence of a peace we cannot create.

This special feature of our consciousness—that allows us to be in relationship with the Presence moment—has many names, none of which really matter. For now, let's call it "conscious awareness." What does matter is to see that, when we are within the field of its active light, everything we are aware of is within us in the same moment. Moreover, *our awareness of the present moment is one and the same as the Presence within us that grants us that awareness.* And while the great promise of this next idea may take a while to understand fully, it is nonetheless true.

This revelation literally points to the entrance of an unthinkably confident relationship with life. The nearer we come to understanding the promise of this insight, the closer we are to knowing a self-command that can't be taken from us. Here's why: The awareness of our living relationship with the present moment—our willingness to consciously practice its presence—empowers us to know what's best for us *without having to think about it.*

This level of awareness *sees* what is real and what is not. Its power to command challenging moments derives from its complete innocence. Higher consciousness doesn't "try" to control events, because its timeless nature is already a partner in guiding creation itself, so what has it to fear? And the more we place ourselves in the presence of this indwelling light, the more we will see small miracles take place before our very eyes. Quiet command over all that unfolds becomes as effortless for us as it is for the spreading light of dawn to chase away morning shadows. An upwelling confidence in the secret goodness of life replaces conflict and self-doubt. After all, how can we fail to find the fearless life we seek when reality itself points the way!

Always remember that all unwanted moments appear accompanied by two forces: a sense of powerlessness and a sense of losing command. But remember as well that anything that tells us to fear some moment or situation has already—by the nature of its own false perception—rendered itself powerless. When we see the truth of this, we drop our unconscious relationship with this fearful level of Self in favor of a quiet awareness of our fearless Self.

Instead of relying on what is powerless to deliver us from what disturbs us—as we've always done in the past—we choose to wake up and practice the Presence! When we do, that dreaded bad dream of feeling powerless in the face of some situation "bigger" than we are can't get started because we quietly refuse to let it start and to render us helpless. When we choose to wake up and practice the Presence, we place ourselves in the presence of a power that ensures our perfect safety.

Remember what is true, act on it, and you will realize the greatest and most priceless gift any human being can ever hope to know—a conscious relationship with that innermost Presence whose celestial nature is fearlessness itself.

Chapter 15

Have the Courage
to Change

Regardless of how one may feel in any given moment, real life can present no task before us for which we are "inadequate."

Yes, we may be unprepared at its outset—just as a leaf-bare late autumn tree can't know, in advance, the weight of a heavy winter snowfall until its branches bend and maybe even break beneath it. But no tree is its limbs, and neither are we made less for what we can't do or carry when first challenged by something that seems too great for us to handle.

Our truest strength lies in our ability to realize that whatever our present weakness may be, it is only temporary, provided we are willing to persist, to wade into what seems greater than we are, and to test this truth time and time again.

The unimaginable reward of persisting through whatever stands in your way is the eventual—the inevitable—discovery of this fundamental truth:

You are not only created to change, you are free to do so anytime you choose!

About the Author

GUY FINLEY lives and teaches in southern Oregon, where he is founder and director of the nonprofit *Life of Learning Foundation*, a world-renowned school of self-realization. He has been helping individuals find a life of uncompromised freedom and enduring fulfillment for thirty years. A modern-day master, Guy Finley is the best-selling author of more than thirty-eight books and unique audio albums, including *The Essential Laws of Fearless Living*, *Let Go and Live in the Now*, *The Secret of Letting Go*, and *Liberate Your Self*.

Visit his foundation online at *www.guyfinley.org* and subscribe to his free weekly e-newsletter.

To write the author about this book, receive information about his ongoing classes, or request a catalog of his works (along with a free helpful study guide), send a self-addressed, stamped envelope to:

Guy Finley
PO Box 10 – CTBF
Merlin, OR 97532
Phone: 541-476-1200

To learn more about Guy's work or *Life of Learning Foundation*, and for a wealth of helpful information, free audio and video downloads, and to request your free starter kit, visit *www.guyfinley.org*.

A special FREE gift for buyers of *The Courage to Be Free*

Harness the Secret Power of Conscious Persistence

A NEW BREAKTHROUGH 60-minute DVD from best-selling author Guy Finley. Includes FREE shipping.*

Guy Finley's powerful new DVD, *Harness the Secret Power of Conscious Persistence,* is a practical step-by-step guide to assuring your success as a human being. Use its wisdom to jump over barriers, dissolve persistent problems, and enjoy the life you really want. Learn the secrets to being bolder, braver, more creative, more peaceful—and how to persist in a special way that ensures you discover the permanent and lasting fulfillment your heart longs for.

- Discover real and lasting peace of mind.

- Understand the nature of true success that can never be taken from you.

- Know a love that transcends fear, worry, and doubt.

- Know the clarity and stillness of your true Self.

- Transform painful troubles into the source of your greatest pleasures.

Don't miss this opportunity to learn how to grow in relationship with the source of true self-liberation. Request your FREE copy of *Harness the Secret Power of Conscious Persistence* by author Guy Finley today.

Visit *www.guyfinley.org/CourageDVD* or call (541) 476-1200 to request your FREE DVD today!

---

* Free shipping offer valid for addresses in the U.S. only. Limited time offer. Subject to change. Please see Web site for further information and restrictions.

Praise for Guy Finley

"A source of inspiration and hope, Guy Finley's *The Courage to Be Free* is recommended for anyone—everyone—navigating life's tricky roads."

—Jordan Rich, WBZ Boston talk host

"Guy Finley has done it again with his powerful teaching metaphors! He is simply the best in the field at describing the 'inside game,' awakening to a higher level of self."

—Stephen Daniel, Ph.D., founder of *QuantumTechniques.com*

"Guy Finley's latest talents in *The Courage to Be Free* will do *just that*—fill your bucket full of practical advice to reach your highest mountain or conquer your most pressing challenge."

—Shelley Irwin, host of the NPR show *The WGVU Morning Show*, Grand Rapids

"What's so unique about *The Courage to Be Free* is how accessible it is. Fun and entertaining stories—parables, really—lead us through each insight so that not only does the information stick, it's instantly absorbed. This is the kind of book you want to keep with you at all times. A joy to read!"

—Anna Darrah, director of acquisitions, Spiritual Cinema Circle

"This book is a very enjoyable ride out of the captivity of limiting misconceptions and into the light of personal freedom."

—Brad Yates, author of *The Wizard's Wish* and coauthor of *Freedom at Your Fingertips*

"In *The Courage to Be Free*, Guy Finley gives us the tools to wake up right now to the Presence that we truly are, free of all false limitations, beliefs, and lies."

—Dr. Sheri Rosenthal, author of *The Complete Idiot's Guide to Toltec Wisdom*, and *Banish Mind Spam!*

"An eloquent instruction manual through which Guy leads us, in his engaging, no-nonsense style, step by step to realizing the promise of his title."

—Jane E. Plotkin, M.A.

"At this pivotal, evolutionary moment in human history, the most necessary teaching is just what Finley suggests—all experiences are opportunities for growth, and we are born with all the spiritual assets needed to meet whatever the future holds."

—Mary Carroll Nelson, author of *Beyond Fear: A Toltec Guide to Freedom and Joy—The Teachings of Don Miguel Ruiz*

"You can't help but come away from this insightful book a better and happier person, and empowered to become free of fear and negativity."

—Gina Lake, author of *Loving in the Moment*

"Guy has done it again! This no-nonsense book shows people how to overcome their fear, helping them to discover and obtain real freedom that will last a whole lifetime . . . and perhaps beyond."

—Linda Mackenzie, founder of *HealthyLife.Net*

"Let go and listen to the inevitable harmony around us. Guy Finley guides us in reflection, resonance, and clarity as we attune to the greatest gift of creation: freedom."

—Don Campbell, musician and author of *Healing at the Speed of Sound* and *The Harmony of Health*

"Guy Finley leads us to our full potential by helping us understand that we must apply the spiritual truths [found in this book] to our life if we are ever to see the transformations we are all seeking."
    —DeDe Murcer Moffett, founder and CEO of Snap
    Out of It! Women's Network

"One of the clearest and most inspiring books I've ever read on practical spirituality."
    —John Seeley M.A., author of *Get Unstuck!*

"*The Courage to Be Free* reminds us that we already have all the tools we need to live a limitless life . . . and teaches us how to use them with expert precision."
    —Chris Cade, author of *Think Without the Box*

"Guy Finley's greatest gift is his brilliant understanding of the truth of who we really are."
    —Dr. Carol Robin, host of Profound Paths to Health,
    Healing and Happiness

"Other than when prompted to by its powerful wisdom to fully comprehend what I was reading, I could not put down Guy Finley's latest incredible book, *The Courage to Be Free*."
    —Scott Cluthe, host and producer of *Positively Incorrect!* radio

"*The Courage to Be Free* lights our way out of smallness and fear and into the steady brilliance of what Guy Finley calls the original Self. Everyone talks about how to 'fight fear.' Reading this book, you discover there is nothing out there to battle with."
    —Andrea Conway, Law of Attraction business coach

"In *The Courage to Be Free*, Guy Finley shakes away our sleep so we might remember the truth of who we really are at the core of our free and authentic self. My advice: read him and heed him!"
    —Greg Willson, editor of *Cultivate Life!* magazine

To Our Readers

WEISER BOOKS, an imprint of Red Wheel/Weiser, publishes books across the entire spectrum of occult and esoteric subjects. Our mission is to publish quality books that will make a difference in people's lives without advocating any one particular path or field of study. We value the integrity, originality, and depth of knowledge of our authors.

Our readers are our most important resource, and we appreciate your input, suggestions, and ideas about what you would like to see published. Please feel free to contact us to request our latest book catalog, or to be added to our mailing list.

Red Wheel/Weiser, LLC
500 Third Street, Suite 230
San Francisco, CA 94107
www.redwheelweiser.com